The Arcane Mechanics
of Constant Lift

poems

Jed Myers

Sheila-Na-Gig Editions

The Arcane Mechanics of Constant Lift © Jed Myers, 2023
Cover Art: Leonardo Da Vinci *Vitruvian Bird*

ISBN: 979-8-9873058-3-6

Sheila-Na-Gig Editions
Russell, KY
Hayley Mitchell Haugen, Editor
www.sheilanagigblog.com

Acknowledgments

I remain grateful to the editors of the publications noted, in which the following poems first appeared.

Another Chicago Magazine: "The Humility of Old Men"
Atticus Review: "Inside the Smoke," "What Was the Queen Anne's Lace"
The Coachella Review: "A Visit"
Cutthroat: "Before Your Mother"
Frontier Poetry: "Unveiling"
The Greensboro Review: "Our Own Thievery"
Innisfree Poetry Journal: "Continuous"
National Poetry Competition Winners' Anthology 2021 and *The Poetry Review*: "I Picture Him Driving"
The Night Heron Barks: "Country Music"
ONE ART: a journal of poetry: "In Common"
Parabola: "A Prayer"
Ruminate: "The Wanting"
Rust + Moth: "Talk at the End of Summer"
The Shore: "Projector," "Rain's Memory"
Solstice: "On the Day of a Distant Invasion"
Southword: "Lastness"
So we go about our days (Winchester Poetry Festival winners' anthology 2021): "The News at Golden Gardens"
Split Rock Review: "Having First Heard of the Ivory-Billed Woodpecker on its Being Pronounced Extinct"
What Rough Beast: "Seclusion Math"

In addition to all those involved in originally publishing some of these poems, my thanks goes to Hayley Mitchell Haugen of Sheila-Na-Gig Editions for her recognition and support of this work, and to others, named or unnamed here, who've facilitated, tolerated, and encouraged the writing and revising of these poems. Heidi Seaborn, Martha Silano, and Tina Schumann have been faithfully catalytic in the development of these pieces. The folks who gather for Easy Speak in Seattle have all been of deep reassurance. My brother Ford has cheered me on with his knowing affirmations. And my co-conspirator in many ventures, Alina Rios, has had her sleeves up with me countless mornings and a good few nights.

I dedicate this collection of poems to the memory of my father,
Jerry Myers, who taught me hope.

Contents

Rain's Memory

It's dark out and I can hear the rain
through an open window, nothing to see
but a few lights haloed in the blur.

The downpour shakes a deep whisper
out of the trees. It could be the sea,
or wind through thick scrub on a bluff.

Could be the sound of time crashing
against life's reef, what we first heard

as blood coursed the new snail shells
of our inner ears. And I remember

my grandmother's bed, her windows
wide on a row of sycamores, a summer
shower—how the leaves roared

lulled me, that noise of the world
the rush and sizzle of surf, a water god's
or a sky god's hand brushing the earth,

a throng cheering its heroes home,
a radio on with no station. I'd float

that sonic ocean on my pillowed raft,
the fighting would go on downstairs,

my bellowing grandfather might strike
my aunt to the kitchen floor, and again
my father, called to the impossible

rescue, his black Buick growling
its harnessed explosions, would pull in
under the mottled boughs. It's all there

in the rain even now. I'm at the sill,
drifting once more to the harsh music,

fusion of countless staccato blows,
the pummeled leaves lifting our wounds.

Having First Heard of the Ivory-Billed Woodpecker on its Being Pronounced Extinct

On the 20th Avenue Bridge, a memory
or flight of imagining: I hear myself
saying *Home* through my spread fingers

sweeping the green deciduous woods
of the ravine. I've got the kid scooped up
in my other arm. He bangs the rail

with the pudgy hand not tugging
my ear. Can he feel our height above
creek bed with his gut sense for falls?

His hoot sounds more like inspiration
for flight, like he might bolt from my grip
or slip free from the nest of his flesh

to rise like the weightless soul he could be
for all I know, out over the canopy
into unfenced expanse now that he sees

where he's from, the horizon cumuli
calling to him like the mountains of home.
Is there music? He's cooing to something.

All I hear is a plane's waning drone
fading south. And those scattered cries
from the branches, sources I can't name

for all my years—winged forms
who could be disappeared before this one
lifts from my arms to find home.

I Picture Him Driving

My father never said lonely. He'd say *Let's*
go to Alfredo's. Soon as he'd collapsed
in the living room chair home from work. We'd see
how beat he was. He'd talk through his yawns,

then he'd thrust himself forward and push
up off the chair's arms, go wrestle
his coat back on, and we'd follow him
out the front door to the car. He would drive

over the limit, slow down for stop signs
or rights on red, and pull a quick left
through a brief gap in City Line's oncoming traffic
to land us in Alfredo's lot. He said *hungry*

at times, never empty. There'd be *caprese*
and *Who else'll have some, come on, don't make me*
finish it all by myself. He'd tell us
again about Italy, say *Next comes the primi,*

he'd have the *risotto* or *gnocchi*, the rest of us
whatever, noodles in red sauce, and after,
keeping the cloth napkin tucked at his neck,
for him the *secondi*, veal, chicken, lobster…

we'd drag our forks through what was left
on our plates. And he'd have put in for several
contorni, the parmesan-graced asparagus
plus a few more to pass around—we'd sample

these for his sake in our fullness. He'd never think
we'd had enough, though we'd be dazed
by the time the *tiramisu* arrived, one for each.
He'd finish his, and at last lifting

the bib from his collar, would ask for the check.
My father never said what was the matter.
He'd take his Alka-Seltzer and Tums
through the night, wind up in front of the TV

in the den before dawn, and head out
in the dark for work. He never said restless,
but I watched his relentless thrashing
in his hospice bed—he wanted to get dressed

and out to the car, saying *Come on let's*
go get the soup. What are we waiting for?
I wonder if that soup was his mother's
winter borsht, roots grounding us once more

in Minsk or Vilnius, but I'm convinced
it was a rich *minestrone*. And evenings I picture him
driving alone in those sun-dried hills of his
heaven, to dine at the next stucco inn.

Blood Water Light

in my grandfather's eyes blinking away
at the dust stirred off the shelves of Ralph's
Army Navy on Market in Wilmington—

mites and specks of lead, tiny paint flecks
and shreds of cardboard, invisible
wisps of the twine he's tied around boxes,
orphan bits of pine left by the saws…all

riding along on his lids' reddened edges
and caught in the wet of that blue-veined shine
the whole way home on the train. He rubs

the heels of his hands into those sockets
and thinks only *tired*. He climbs the long stairs,
enters the echoes of 30th Street Station's
grand concourse, and exits close under

the tall wings of a bronze Archangel Michael
lifting a soldier from the world. He finds
his tailfinned Dodge in its film of Philadelphia

grime, and drives to 60th & Cedar
for a late dinner of left-over fish
in the kitchen. He lights a drugstore cigar,
sips instant decaf my grandmother brings him,

and drags ashen smoke like more dust
down his windpipe just like the doc says *don't
it'll kill you one night*. Tonight I'm looking

into the blood water light of his dust-
scoured eyes, into that huffing torrent of his
love's effort, that rude spitting immigrant
thick-hearted oxygen-thirsty current

of him, who churns through the dust
for us toward the shore till breath gives out
ahead where that gleaming surf scrubs.

Long Love
—for A

How could I not sing blessings of days
with you? A thousand camellias now
throwing deep-pink skirts up at the shy light

on the canal, I see it might've been
fine had I made no such sounds till now,
but thrill and thanks pry my lips wide

and out spills a voice with no language
to dress it. *I love you*? That's not prayer
enough for this breath—it would leave love

wound on itself like the wintered wisteria
leafless and snagged to the porch. So I mutter
skyward, or into my pillow, or some mornings

through the window as if to inform
the Japanese maple that eavesdrops on life
in the house—praise I know not to aim

for your face. Strange? No more than ancient
men bowing in rote devotions in a *shul*
my grandfather showed me. Even like those

lowered eyes of yours in the bar's jostle
when we first stumbled close and I felt it,
I'd known you, and wanted to sing for you

in that original tongue, what we'd whispered
in some *shtetl* orchard that might still bear apples
in this world. So I keep blooming

my ersatz Yiddish, Hebraic gibberish,
faux Aramaic—senseless petals tossed
into the open to float past your ears—

like the refrains my soul's throat sang
before, in cloud-light slant-beamed on a river,
in blood-and smoke-scented piney gusts, sang

long as I could till one war or another
hurled its axe into the earth between us.
Now I sing my nonsense in your presence

daily—you may pick up an old strain,
then you'll know us, and know you've seen
our bodies torched, how we've scavenged

roots and trust and found in each other's
arms sweet refuge. No words for our lives—
love thrives scorched, scattered, crushed.

Unveiling

My brother and I idle by the plot. I spot our mother
stirring the rolled oats again in the light of the old kitchen
window. She coughs, still clearing her chest of the smoke

she welcomed into her lungs last night. Smog's gathered
around her heart. She's dying, I know, to cry a loud
curse, but we are her new life on our twin stools

at the wooden counter, our hungry bowls before us
like alms cups, and if she can't swallow her dark flares
and feed us, fear is she'll become what she hates

of this long dry valley she's traveled, coal hills to city
to city, her father long dead of a curse in his bowels,
her husband out there in the beams of the day's adulations,

her mother a full day away by train and decreeing
the distance calls for *No tears* on the phone—I blink
into our new polished window of stone as she strikes

the rim of the pot again with the neck of that spoon,
the lean winter light on her yellow terrycloth robe
like the thin glow of a new season. I listen—the tin-drum

repeat through the white steel of the stove the unsettled
question of weeping's welcome, then through the dark
grating of her carved name, I hear the spoon scraping.

Projector

I'd curl the film around the bright sprockets,
seat the square holes onto those metal teeth,
and thread the celluloid over the glass plate
behind the lens, so the beam could project
the frame-by-frame story onto the sparkling
screen I'd stretched and hooked up in front
of the class. It wasn't a job I liked.
It was to discover I'm not made for tech.
I did take to wondering, while the rest watched
in the dark, while bicycle safety was modeled
by smiling ghost-kids on their silvery roads,
while Jascha Heifetz attempted to thrill us
again with his bow, or gray combines ripped up
wide rows of wheat for our airy white bread,
wondering, then, about what gets projected,

presented, inserted, fed…. I'm wondering
these nights again, the lamps off, screen lit
with snippets on fires, the plague, my need
to take turmeric daily, the web's own selection
of swimsuits just the right fit for my love,
and swarms of warnings, more than I can heed,
uprisings yeasted left and right, the next
wild contagion pitching its warm-ups
in some Central-Asian bullpen, predictions
Wyoming's caldera will eat the American
West, an asteroid's aiming to knock us off
orbit, and dare I not password-protect
my passwords, what then. My stinging eyes lick
the salt of the alerts. Whatever I click on
brings on more spin, and I'm in my dust devils,

sucking at scandals, yes choking a bit
on the whirling particulates, still swilling
the whirlwind. I imbibe revelations
as if they were heaven-light, herbed medicinal
akvavit shots, blood-cleanser, swiggable
tincture of anticipation in this creaking
room whose walls flicker with the world's
glinting sharp instruments. I do remember

the soothe of that insistent clicking I liked to get
lost in beside the projector, that hyper-quick
metronome keeping time for the dancing
picture, a ticking brisk as the frictionless
flourish and trill of Yehudi Menuhin's
black-and-white violin the machine launched
into the chalk-dusted air. I'd look

into the beam where it widened between
the bulb-shine and that illumined rectangle,
to witness the aimless flecks, that floating grit
scintillant like early clumps of the cosmos
drawn to our star, first mineral stuff
of the unformed Earth—I'd have that sense
of before, before any thought, before a myth
brought an army of nomads together, or a mind
found the Hunter Orion out there in a cluster
of stars nowhere near each other. Tonight,
I wonder about all the lost minds clicking
on warnings they want or need to just hold
their lives together. The little screens offer
an incessant feed on the demons among us.
What would it be, to thrive on raw wonder?

Isn't there room in the void around all things
visible, room wider than the fields
where Orion paces and waits? Space for more
doubt and hope than our whole hoard of beliefs?
I'll step out tonight, lose the Hunter, see
if I can erase the names Rigel and Bellatrix,
drop the belt and sword, gather the beams,
and muse on what presses a human creature
to swallow the spores of alarm, to stiffen
and point, to pipe a strained conviction
the throat constricts to a whine, to curse viral
visions of child-abductors, blood-harvesters,
world-ensnarers.... I'm wondering how
the projection mechanics and circuitry work.
The wetware must be just like mine.

Country Music

I'd stand on a flat rock low to the river,
cast over the eddies, drop the lure
into fast water, reel to keep the hook
off the bottom, and feel for a strike.

Up there out of the buzz of my city
Sundays—where the Sultan runs
under twin bridges, railway and Route 2,
to join the Skykomish—I'd hear the deep

drone of the mountain runoff's tons
gushing over the stones, that incessant
crash on the riverbed's hidden ridges,
the high tones broadcast off the crests

fringed with foam, that churn working
oxygen down to the fish. It was often
the kids came with. One autumn the older
hauled in a Coho. I remember it

flipping itself, sides red as the vine maple
spread on the opposite shore, one eye
after the other on blank blue sky
till the boy conked it. That shudder

we'd seen before, a few seconds,
and it was no trouble to pull the hook.
With or without a catch, we would roll
back with our blood full of that country

music, that rush in our veins,
the shiver of snowmelt in our spines.
Sometimes I'd hear a dull knock
from below—the river turning a rock.

Before Your Mother

—for the "Naked Athena" of Portland, July 19, 2020

That nakedness we two tykes were allowed
to revel in, hot afternoons in the round
inflatable pool on the lawn, shallow bright
plastic pond our mom firmed up for us
with her magic smoke-scented breaths,

that nakedness of our pallor susceptible
to the sear of the ultraviolet, before
the first bad burn on the Jersey Shore, before
the pleasure of all our splashes and squeals went
quiet inside our embarrassment,

that nakedness we jumped up in to go run
around on the radiant grass, before
we ever felt stripped of a thing—yes I think
it was an age, hazy as it remains
in its blur of elation—it was no dressing-down,

that nakedness. Did the shine on the taut yellow
skin of the pool in the sun seem a touch
lurid to us even then? We had begun
sorting sensations. The water cool
on our legs, bottoms, genitals, something

that nakedness meant, meant again
when we lifted into the air and a wind cooled us
further. Was there a hint of shame blowing
over the hedge? A war somewhere? Our garden
seemed a wide-enough world. And it was

that nakedness—under the blue approval
of an eternal summer sky, joyful
as we were at our palms' plash
on the give and soothe of that fluid glass—
that we'd learn to cover. Exactly

that, nakedness under the button-down
shirt, slid into twin tubes of cuffed khaki
pants, the ticklish nudity of our toes
tucked into socks and shoes, our hearts
curtained behind team logos, and soon

that nakedness tied and jacketed, disavowed
religion of our original trust—
this is the cost of a roof, a car, a desk
job that could go somewhere. This, the cover-up
of what we are—we come across clips of

that nakedness. The long lines of Jews
who've arrived, undressed, and had their heads
shaved, readied to have their arms
tattooed; the Vietnamese girl who's run
out of her Napalm-incinerated clothes…

that nakedness, in the prisons, of black boys
being shown for the ten-thousandth last time
who's boss. It isn't always, but it is so
often, the pale numb skin of the man
with the club, the gun, and the authority over

that nakedness hides in a uniform. I saw,
in Portland, a line of the president's men,
masked and helmeted, oddly in desert-tan
camo, ready to fracture a few locals'
bones, when a fleshy Athena sat down in

that nakedness, in the open before those men,
her soft skin on the macadam, arms and legs
spread, and her timeless form said *Remember
boys, your wet glee in the garden? You're naked
before me now as before your mother then.*

Lastness

Time I confess, right here, under
the branches of this naked katsura,
its malty death scent in the air—

now while I'm surrounded by evidence
I couldn't help it. Not this autumn,
the Japanese maple in its fatal flare,

freeway's blue roar a mournful rage,
allure of pure formlessness in the haze....
I mouth a word for it all that isn't quite

right—too bitter and I want to spit
and I wince to picture my grimacing
listener who isn't anyone yet.

And will anyone imagine this planet
a woman whose typhoon whisper starts
in her throat the magma conduits?

And her lips all the parts that can touch
other parts—raindrops and bullets,
gale-blasts against breakwaters, worn

fingernails scratching at walls? She
also isn't coming up with the right
word. But as the sea's storms'

great speaker cones wail, the fires'
crests crescendo over the foothill
developments, the gunrunners run

our young into the ground, the bees
cease in the dirt, the orcas go bony,
and knowing the white bear drowns—

I admit to it. Even these brown leaves
crinkling in swells at my feet
now chime like the highest bells

and radiate their unsealed brilliance.
What's a word for this, world shining
her first face through life's dying?

A Visit

This other light she's wrapped in
lifts the furrows life left in her
skin. All her ages now,

or none—no shadow where
she leans at something like a desk.
Her dark pen streams an ink-

black shine along the vein-blue
lines down one white page
then the next. The letters weave

like seaweed in a tide-swept river
mouth. Silent lips move
with her hand—a kind of speech.

I start to wake, to drift
between two lands. She couldn't
see me, and I couldn't read.

Parthenogenesis

...the rhyme or reason for its occurrence in the condors remains an enigma.
    —Isaac Schultz, in *Gizmodo*, October 28, 2021

They certainly weren't, shall we say, shining specimens...
    —Demian Chapman, Mote Marine Laboratory and Aquarium

Both perished young, one in a zoo
    of a foot infection, the other starved
in the wild. No, not *shining*

specimens of the black-feathered clan
    whose lean hunters clean the land of the dead.
Whose soaring wings span more than the height
    of a man. Long-lived

monk-bald tribe, beak-faces painted
    red for their funereal feasts,
genes on the edge, as among lizards

or some catsharks or the occasional chicken,
    two were found to have hatched with no father
in them. Magnificent twist—what turn

of the helix is this? Press of a current
    we've got no monitors for? Work
of a wandering force we don't know

is there to measure? Are there fine strings
    we've missed since we gave the sky over
to that invisible huge-fisted king?
    I wave my hand through the air

so I might feel the delicate tug
    of the web between stars and seeds,
the pull of angels' eyes on my knees.

Or a mother wind sifts through the fingers
    of condors' wings on the valley updrafts,
combs the desiccated sand and its lead-poisoned
    carrion, then flies to the desolate

ova, hisses life into and swells them
    with dust-livening hope, and across
the parched wastes, sows the starts.

In Common

I woke wanting to dig, not for anything
underground, no need for a spade,

and not with some rude analytical
blade to cut through the crust of a mood,

no pickaxing a tomb for artifacts
still in the dust of a dead adolescence,

no, this morning, hearing the crows
bickering over where to get breakfast

while they took turns disturbing a puddle
the rain left last night, while I watched

at an open window, a robin waiting
at a safe distance to go wash its wings

once the crows finished and flapped off,
and in that quiet the wind's come-and-go

musings in the tall throat of the maple,
I wanted to dig shallow, for what we hold

in common, just under a feather
coat as under my skin, in the cackle

and chirp as in mutter, in the jackets
you and I wear out the door some hope

some fear in our throats, in our pockets
a little cash scared up for a coffee

and snack at the stand. We might risk
a nod without seeing the other's life.

The Wanting

The wanting, I felt I saw in the dark
brown beetle working its way toward the shining
eye of the good size rabbit dead
on its side by the trail, the wanting

in how that tiny-legged disc of an insect
climbed through what for it was the rough
heath of the rabbit's cheek, the wanting

gone only hours out of the rabbit,
its stillness off its feet and its tolerance
for the bug any live paw would bat at
my evidence for that fresh lack of wanting,

coat still smooth, unnamable color
of the earth's cover of dead leaf mulch
the rabbit must've been suited for, wanting

its life as a body, as my body wants
mine, as the little live coin
of the beetle moved just a thumbnail's width
in the moment I watched—it must be one wanting

life, the sheen-shielded beetle, the legless pale
feasters sure to inch in by the night,
the child I was at the milk of my wanting

I sucked and sucked in the unbroken
weaving of mothers and fathers, all the way
back to the sun-simmered broth of life—
I thought, the hunting, the blades, the wanting

to kill anything to eat and breathe, must be
inseparable from our love, and I lifted
my eyes, past the trees, to the road's drumming.

Our Own Thievery

The bed squealed on us to the shadows
of our getaway. We whispered, laughed,
and let the daylight's inquest go on
delivering its indictments to the trees,

the rooftops, the glass towers, tent-dwellers
working the ramps, all the bright hulls
drifting the blacktop canals—the sun's
floodlight on the easy evidence, while we lay

low in our cove. Sure, we noticed
the curtains, shifty in the open window.
And we overheard that soft flip-flop
testimony of the fabric on frame and sash.

Hints of wind reached in like the murmurs
of a courthouse crowd. The air knew
where to find us. But why now do I spin it
this way? We'd made off with the timeless

gem of an hour, till the light fell
and a chill slipped in. We were even granted
a sweet release, and when we walked
from each other after, it felt like free will.

So, let the record show we'd done nothing—
nothing, though while entangled together
we'd heard the volcanic dad two doors down
erupting again—we'd gone on

teasing sighs and moans and simple words
from each other. Had we registered
any of those sirens that keep calling
out of the University District? We hadn't

thought the loose fence slat's slaps could be
gunfire down there. Well, look at us,
in no way impaired, just heartsick
with our own thievery—we stole the day,

licking the light off each other's shoulders.
And we'd siphon the stars down our throats.

The News at Golden Gardens

Osaka's doctors have run low
    on the propofol to sedate
the breathless they must intubate.

*

    Turtles repose on the pond's logs
though it isn't sunny. A duckling
    scuttles over the planked walkway.

*

In Maharashtra, surgeons take black-
    fungus-colonized eyes from those
who otherwise will die.

*

    Today the tide's risen close
enough to reach the nearest
    of the ghost-pier's bleached posts.

*

Where, ever, isn't here? In Gaza,
    how will the bone-shaken rise
from their new era of stones?

*

    And here, on a taken inland
sea and its land, crows slash the wind,
    hawks hold drifts above the trees,

*

and a freight train groans in
    from south to somewhere, lugging,
God knows, what they need there.

Talk at the End of Summer

All my three offspring in town for the last
of August, we potluck into the dusk
on the weathered deck, big Japanese maple
leaning its reddened breeze-shivered leaves
and samaras over us as if to eavesdrop.

Low in the plum-purple southeast, Saturn
grants us an audience. The kids, grown
and partnered, talk of not having kids—no
little round mouths irresistibly calling
for more rice or milk than there is, no new
throats in the drought, and no pink lungs
panting for oxygen while it runs out.

I see the loose ends of my lineage, bloomless
stems, sprouts swept useless across clay
hardpan—our uncanny design gone
fruitless. There won't be a miracle
miniature hand come to clutch my thumb, no
pair of womb-fresh wide eyes ushering
a jaundiced old one back into love's home.

So let it be these young, whose genes
have swum eons on a rough tide of births
wanted and not. Let Saturn see these
thoughtful ones, faces dusky as the rose
petals fallen along the fence, eyes casting
moon-like light before moonrise, lips
reposed between soft-spoken reflections....

Let my awe show as these once little ones
discuss the loss of their intricate code.
Will Saturn bless them? Can these dangling
seed-wings hear? Does anything earthly
remember? I'm kissing each child goodnight.

Inside the Smoke

Not a sky, a milk of ash—no,
more like a low clay dome

on just these few houses, cars,
snippet of the street, the near

trees...we're down to earshot.
Suppose no Jupiter in the south

tonight. No moon. World gone
small inside the smoke. Might be

a hope—to know close quarters.
Mosquito's, pangolin's, vole's,

water strider's—all this round
garden, sky-bound, islet, dot.

Katsura, maple, that backyard
Sequoia with its height erased...

a squirrel's circuit. A snail's
range. That golden spider's

threads—oasis strung between
two fence slats. And the shaking

yellow jacket wrapped inside
a tiny hanging storm of silk,

a few feet from that wide-
open late white rose.

What Was the Queen Anne's Lace

October's entered wearing a scent,
a blend of wood smoke, hint of late rose
and tattered lavender, that burnt-latex

aroma left when a kid's peeled off after
slamming the door, rain-damp tobacco
smolder, fresh rot of fallen apples—

she must hope we'll at least nod to her
if not bow, not just turn to another
calendar picture of autumn's gold aspens,

not simply gearshift the nerves to type 10
for the month. To not fall for the name
but into the body and breath, the long light

playing the wakes of ducks on the pond
between the stadium and the lake. To stop
and honor the battered heads of the rushes.

To look out across the landfill flats,
sundown rust on the countless brown cones
of what was the Queen Anne's lace, ragged

and leaning together like spent exiles
right where they've thrived. They're brittle
and quietly click in the gusts. October,

camp where a vanished moon will return
to bless the wind-shaken twigs, here,
where summer'd spread a sharp pennyroyal

odor around the pond's rim, I draw in
hard through the nostrils, the summer spell
gone. All the young ducks are grown

and proud in their squabbles. Here she is,
October or Winterfylleth or god knows
what to call her. My shoes in her mud,

I'm half-wishing October were somebody
else. I'm part back before the smoke,
before September's drop ceiling of ash,

and part drawn to a new month's perfume,
lingering char in the air, whiff of muck,
mix of spores, ozone of the imminent

storm, fragrance of worms, and the notes
my nose can't detect, a Coho somewhere
nearby in an osprey's grip, close

as a coyote must be seizing a rabbit
from under the dusk-umber cover of wild
carrot. October stretches before me,

the brush turns velvet, and I breathe her
incense of reckon and loss into my own
slow wreck of muscle and bone. October,

what are we to lay to rest? I hear a siren
crossing the lake bridge. I inhale first
leaf-dust—I'm lost in your ocher dress.

The Humility of Old Men

climbs in through the soles of their feet

might gout a big toe might turn
an ankle whose ligament got loosed up
years ago under a basket

                          might wear
through the cartilage of a right knee

on its way to a hip's ball
                          and socket
and on from there

                  it'll flaccid
the groin's passion gear find a pocket
of bowel to inflame

                    it will infiltrate
the diaphragm and make camp in the heart

tighten the arteries stiffen the lungs
and steepen the hills

                    it will ascend
and drill itself into the pulp of teeth

pull down the shoulders brittle the neck
cloud the eyes yellow the world
                          humility

shrinks old men sometimes to a ripeness
a friends-with-death kind of translucence

lets us see the well-traveled child
who smiles at me from his hospital bed

Seclusion Math

Let us count, but not number,

the embraces before.

       Count the imagined

kisses, let them speed through the clouds to reach
just those lips, cheeks, brows

they were sent for.

       Let us count now,

with no accounting, the moments our arms will fly
round one another in August,

          though we can't
be sure.

     And count, without tally,

those quick subtle starts of the hand
toward love's faces across towns, ranges,

even across the edge of breath.

         Let's count each

touch between hearts, whether or not
we can sense it, every spark or harmonic,

flicker, hint in the air,

       like a small bird's dark

flash across vision's border. Count all our care.

Not Far to Mariupol

This mind in its watery nest,
back from a night's dream sweep, blinks

twin lenses open on a dim room. I've flown
in from a distance. Entered through window

glass on the soft screech of a small bird
and into an ear's funnel, home

from remote lands, times, far
from the possible. A dead friend live,

his fingers still singing through a piano,
just sweeter, sadder. Has he been practicing?

And my mother, weeping at last, allowed me
to hold her. I was well past halfway

around this world. Farther than a radio
wave's bounce off the ozone down

into the tunnel hive by the Sea of Azov.
To who's left alive in that pummel,

minds too rattled to lift on dream.
That's not far. A few wingbeats is all.

On the Day of a Distant Invasion

Down through a forested gouge in the earth,
we took the trail under tall firs and cedars
toward our secret lookout. We wanted to take in
the distances over our inland sea.

Off that water an icy wind infiltrated
our slice of woods—old conifers shifted,
moaned like live sirens. Ferns thrived on those
moss-curtained towers—countless fronds waved
like green warning flags.

              We kept on
and emerged on the ledge where fast air blasted
our faces. We pulled our collars up and our hats
snug. Past the drop-off, twin sheen of tracks
hugging the shore, no train, but the wind gave
a rumbling.

           And all along that unbroken
stretch of stony bare beach, the waves advanced
toward us off that coarse disturbance of sea
with nothing out past it but what seemed the dark
flank of a beast where horizon belonged,

                     waves
in their pale chaos epaulettes, the next
crest and the next, sacrificing themselves down
to froth on the gravel.

           While we stood far
from that edge, and the hoarse din of the front
blowing in filled our ears, I swear we could hear
those swells crash the pebbles, that ceaseless
assault, yes, every last gurgle and hiss.

Putin's Gift

Because we know one warlord can turn the world
into a galaxy of trashcan fires

before the next full moon, this is our chance
to learn fast, now—how well can we love.

Because his cash-hoarders of course only bask
on decks in Dubai as the air burns to unbreathable,

let's inhale and our eyes adore the smudged sky.
Because the leveling's noise will be deafening,

followed by a silence like a neon beer sign buzzing
over the bartender in his blot of dried blood, let's

swell to the twenty instruments still in those hands
playing their best "Ode to Joy" on Maidan Square.

Because the old spymaster has all his murders
chalked up on the insides of his bones, and he knows

the least capitulation would twist him forever
in the piano wires that tether him to those souls,

and because that boyish-looking madman will cross
any threshold to mute the music of our love, let's

cherish one another's breaths, breath
by breath in the dense shadow of the cataclysm. Let's

thrill to all we see of Earth this last day, soft
sheen of skunk cabbage clean up through the spring

muck, pink rug of blown-down camellia
petals across the walkway, the lone robin

standing on that radiance and pulsing out its bold
hope's notes, the bright star magnolia's

stars starting to unfold, and a gust's layered
chorus you'd never have tuned to if not for

the sense this sense-light might now be blown out.

Offering

It'll be *someone*, an evening you're more than half-
gone with loss, gone enough you can hear
the cottonwoods' judgments, and the crow crowd's
jeers from the alders, until *someone* comes.

Before you even notice, *someone* sits down
and faces you, knees almost touching yours,
you feel that interstellar remoteness
and intimate presence at once—it starts

the fragments shaking loose. All the pieces
you've felt stabbing at your insides, they rise
out your mouth, slip from the brims of your eyes, fall
like shining crumbs of glass from your ears

in the slant light. That face, familiar but whose? It's
someone who reads your brokenness, who's heard
the shatter-bits grinding, sniffed the silicate
dust that's wafted out of your lungs.

Between you and *someone* the glittering shrapnel
seems to melt. Was it ice? *Someone* offers
water cupped in joined palms. You'll drink.
Not bitter not sweet, you inhale a hint

of cold mineral creek-bottom, of that granite-bed
brook where you hunted newts as a kid.
And as you breathe deeper, as if you're back
kneeling in maple leaf shade in that gully's mud

behind the brick houses, you look up
at what must be the tint of dusk that's always
settling on us. *Someone*'s gone. Sunset's own wings
open to the edge of the world. You'll go on.

A Prayer

A cormorant crosses a harbor low,
wings' pulse keeping an air pillow
on the bird's shadow, that black
belly a steady few inches aloft.

I know a soft blaze glows
in that dark fuselage. Fine fire courses
a delicate wire web to maintain
the arcane mechanics of constant

lift. A nameless attunement
in that sleek breast resets the ratio
heartbeat to wingbeat, pump's clap
matching the instant's requirement.

That fire's quiet, discrete. We spread
our flame out in whatever gods' names.
Our heat breaches containment.
We spark the wind with bright sticks.

I watch from an edge of the land
we've lit. I see the cormorant
reach a buoy and stand, wings held
wide to the air, a trusting, a prayer.

Continuous

I give the emptiness in my chest to the sky,
sparks in my head to the night, although
I earmark the light in my eyes for the sand
of bay floors where the flounders live.
May my bones' tiny archways coalesce
in the cool tunnels dug under border walls.
I donate the wishes caught in my throat
to the tongues of kids on hot streets. Songs
in orbit around my heart should be flung
360 to seed the musings of tent-dwellers
alongside the freeways. I send my longings
to fluff up the froth in the heads of beers
in the nowhere-from-here taverns. I offer
my summers' joys to clear the airways
of little allergic and asthmatic coughers.
Let my horrors add shine to the spiderwebs
toddlers and cats find under end tables.
And may all my spaces return to continuous
with the full breadth of the world. The rest,
the atoms, can play life or dust as they will.

About the Author

Jed Myers is author of *Watching the Perseids* (Sacramento Poetry Center Book Award), *The Marriage of Space and Time* (MoonPath Press), and, forthcoming, *Learning to Hold* (Wandering Aengus Press Editors' Award). Recent writing appears or is forthcoming in *Rattle, The Poetry Review, RHINO, The Greensboro Review, Rust + Moth, Terrain.org, On the Seawall, The National Poetry Review, Nimrod International Journal,* and elsewhere. Myers lives in Seattle, where he edits the journal *Bracken*.

Sheila-Na-Gig Editions